This

*Annual*

belongs to

........................................................................................................

........................................................................................................

# EGMONT
*We bring stories to life*

First published in Great Britain in 2019 by Egmont UK Limited
The Yellow Building, 1 Nicholas Road, London W11 4AN

Content written and adapted by Helen Archer and Jude Exley

Designed by Elaine Wilkinson

© 2019 Disney Enterprises, Inc

ISBN 978 1 4052 9426 3
70380/001

Printed in Italy

Parental guidance is advised for all craft and colouring activities. Ask an adult to help when using glue, paint and scissors. Wear protective clothing and cover surfaces to avoid staining.

Stay safe online. Egmont is not responsible for content hosted by third parties.

Egmont takes its responsibility to the planet and its inhabitants very seriously.  We aim to use papers from well-managed forests run by responsible suppliers.

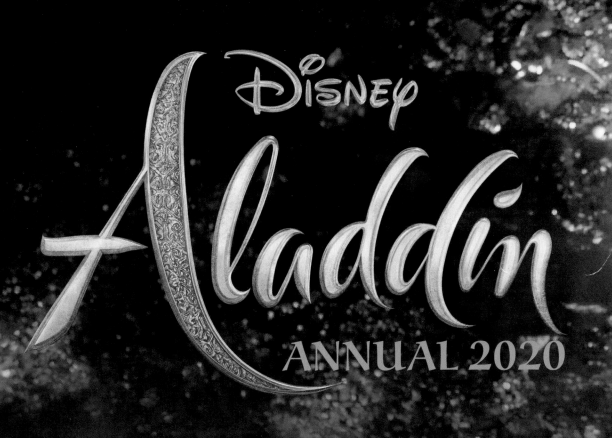

# DISNEY
# Aladdin
## ANNUAL 2020

# Contents

# Get to Know... Aladdin

🪔 *Aladdin* is an orphan who has grown up on the streets of Agrabah.

🪔 He is very resourceful and with his pet monkey, Abu, takes what he needs to survive.

🪔 *Aladdin* dreams of living a better life so he is easily convinced by Jafar to go into the cave to get the lamp.

🪔 He saves *Princess Jasmine* from trouble with a street seller in the market.

🪔 *Aladdin* pretends to be Prince Ali to impress *Jasmine*. The Genie encourages Aladdin to just be himself, but he doesn't realise this at first.

# Magic Carpet Ride

Help Aladdin choose the right path to bring Jasmine a beautiful lotus flower.

1 2 3

Answers on page 69

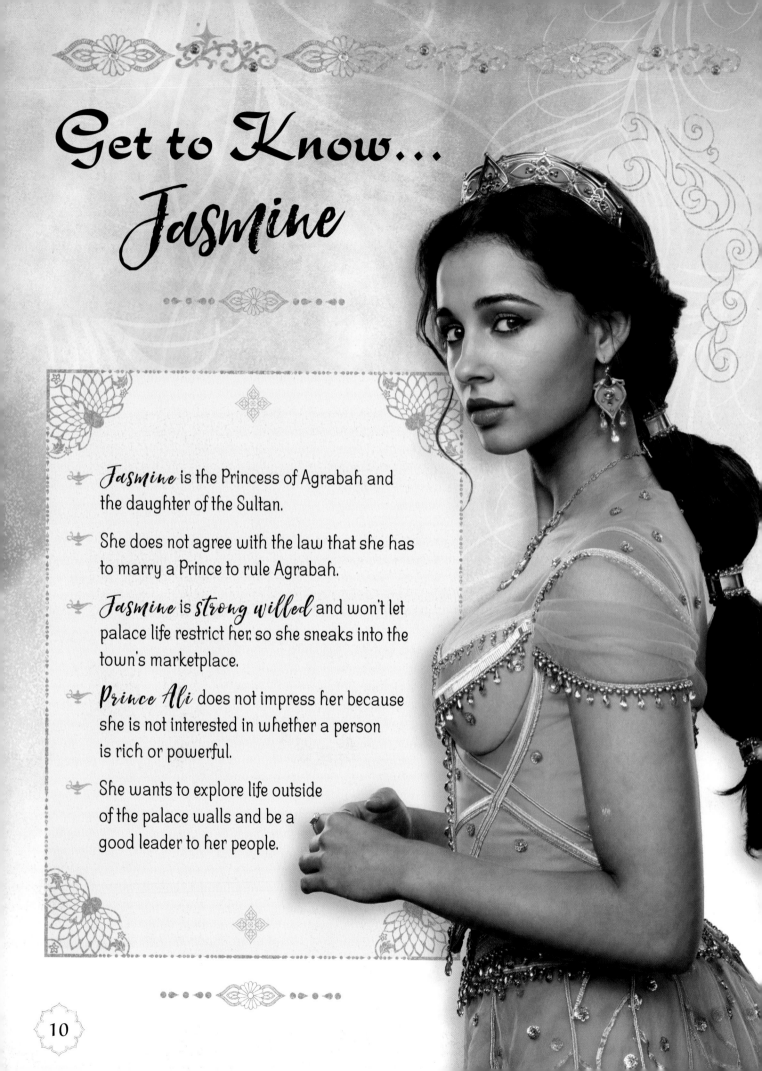

# Get to Know...
## Jasmine

- *Jasmine* is the Princess of Agrabah and the daughter of the Sultan.

- She does not agree with the law that she has to marry a Prince to rule Agrabah.

- *Jasmine* is **strong willed** and won't let palace life restrict her, so she sneaks into the town's marketplace.

- *Prince Ali* does not impress her because she is not interested in whether a person is rich or powerful.

- She wants to explore life outside of the palace walls and be a good leader to her people.

# Follow Your Dreams

If I had one wish, I would . . .

...................................................................................

...................................................................................

I hope that someday I can . . .

...................................................................................

...................................................................................

One way I would change the world is . . .

...................................................................................

...................................................................................

Today I can . . .

...................................................................................

...................................................................................

Tomorrow I want to . . .

...................................................................................

...................................................................................

In the future, I will . . .

...................................................................................

# Get to Know...
## Genie

- *Genie* is the magical friend of *Aladdin*.

- He is a loyal and kind friend who helps *Aladdin* to understand the true meaning of friendship.

- He is bound to the *gold lamp* he lives in, until he is granted freedom by a master.

- *Genie* has great power.

- Aladdin meets Genie in the *Cave of Wonders* when Aladdin rubs the magic lamp.

# Mystical Shadows

Can you spot the shadow that matches this picture of Genie?

A

B

C

D

E

F

Answers on page 69

13

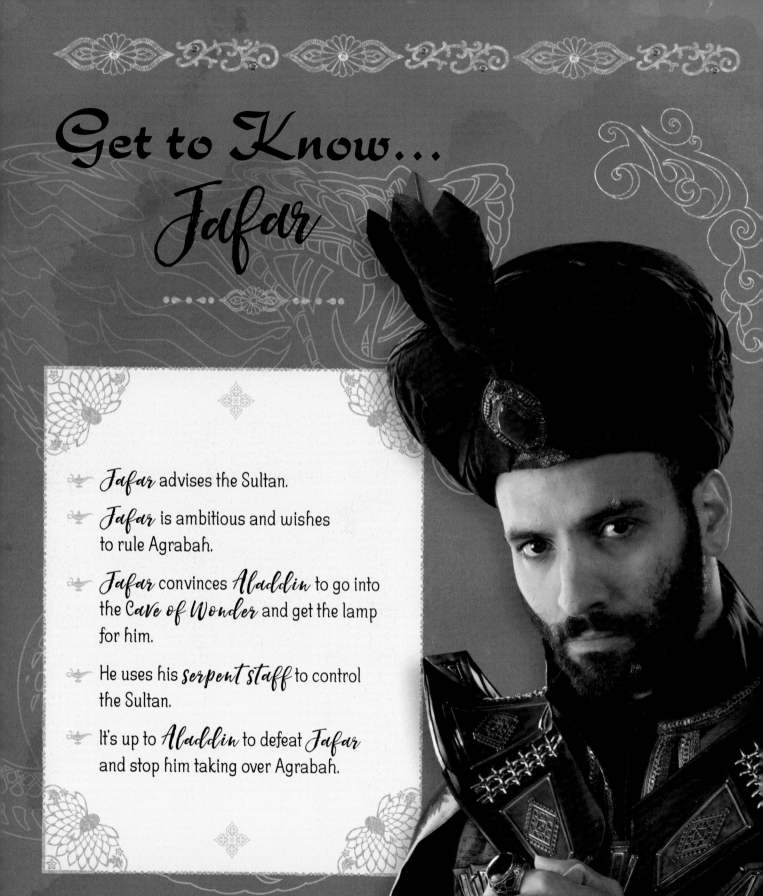

# Get to Know...
## Jafar

- *Jafar* advises the Sultan.

- *Jafar* is ambitious and wishes to rule Agrabah.

- *Jafar* convinces *Aladdin* to go into the *Cave of Wonder* and get the lamp for him.

- He uses his *serpent staff* to control the Sultan.

- It's up to *Aladdin* to defeat *Jafar* and stop him taking over Agrabah.

# Sorcerer's Sudoku

Use your powers to help Jafar complete these sudoku puzzles. There should be one of each picture in every row for each grid.

1

2

3

Answers on page 69

# Get to Know...
# The Royal Palace

* ✦ **The Sultan** is the ruler of Agrabah and the father of **Princess Jasmine**.

* ✦ He believes that Agrabah should be ruled with tradition and stability which **Jasmine** doesn't always agree with.

* ✦ He loves his daughter immensely and only wants the best for her.

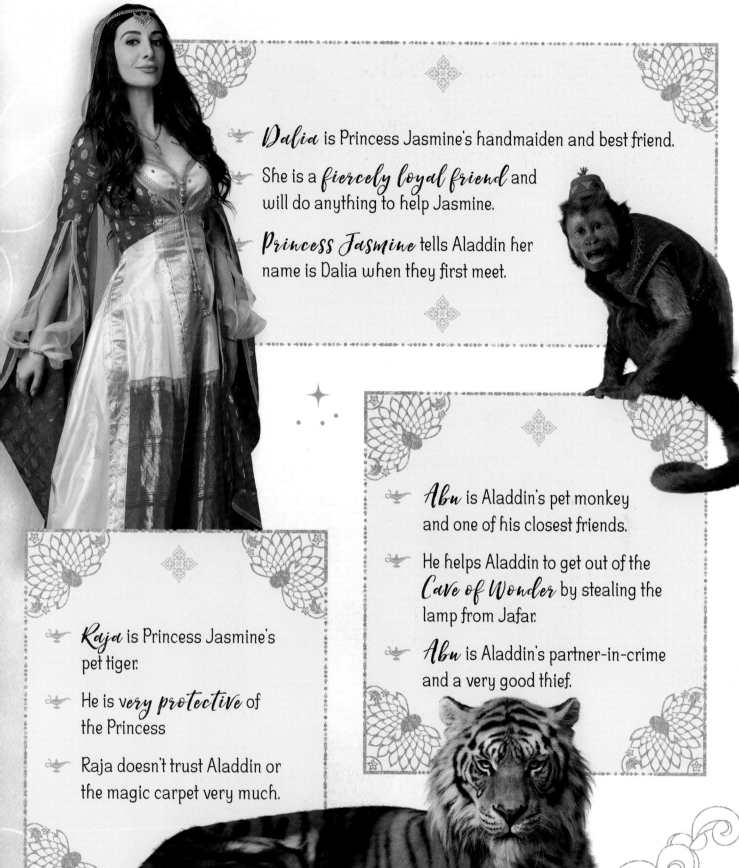

**Dalia** is Princess Jasmine's handmaiden and best friend.

She is a **fiercely loyal friend** and will do anything to help Jasmine.

**Princess Jasmine** tells Aladdin her name is Dalia when they first meet.

**Abu** is Aladdin's pet monkey and one of his closest friends.

He helps Aladdin to get out of the **Cave of Wonder** by stealing the lamp from Jafar.

**Abu** is Aladdin's partner-in-crime and a very good thief.

**Raja** is Princess Jasmine's pet tiger.

He is **very protective** of the Princess

Raja doesn't trust Aladdin or the magic carpet very much.

# Part One

Deep in a desert on the outskirts of Agrabah, a mysterious man named Jafar sent a thief into the Cave of Wonders. Jafar knew that only a 'diamond in the rough' could get him the magical gold lamp inside. But as the cave mouth closed, Jafar realised that he still hadn't found the right person.

Meanwhile, on the streets of Agrabah, a young man named Aladdin and his pet monkey Abu, were exploring the marketplace. They often found items that others had lost or misplaced and kept these trinkets for themselves. But today they found someone special ...

On the other side of the marketplace, a beautiful young woman was walking between the stalls. Little did anyone know that she was Princess Jasmine, the daughter of the Sultan of Agrabah. She had sneaked out of the palace to see more of the kingdom, but got into trouble with a stall owner. Luckily, Aladdin saw this and helped her. They ran into one of the buildings and onto the rooftop.

# "Do you trust me?"

Aladdin asked Jasmine. She nodded and followed him across the city's rooftops to his secret hideaway in the top of an abandoned tower.

Safe in the tower, Aladdin and Jasmine introduced themselves. Wanting to keep her identity a secret, Jasmine told Aladdin that her name was Dalia.

When Jasmine heard trumpets blowing, she knew it was time to go back to the palace, but as she left, she realised Aladdin had her bracelet and thought he must be a thief.

Back in his hideaway, Aladdin discovered the bracelet Abu had stolen. He knew he must sneak into the palace and return it to her.

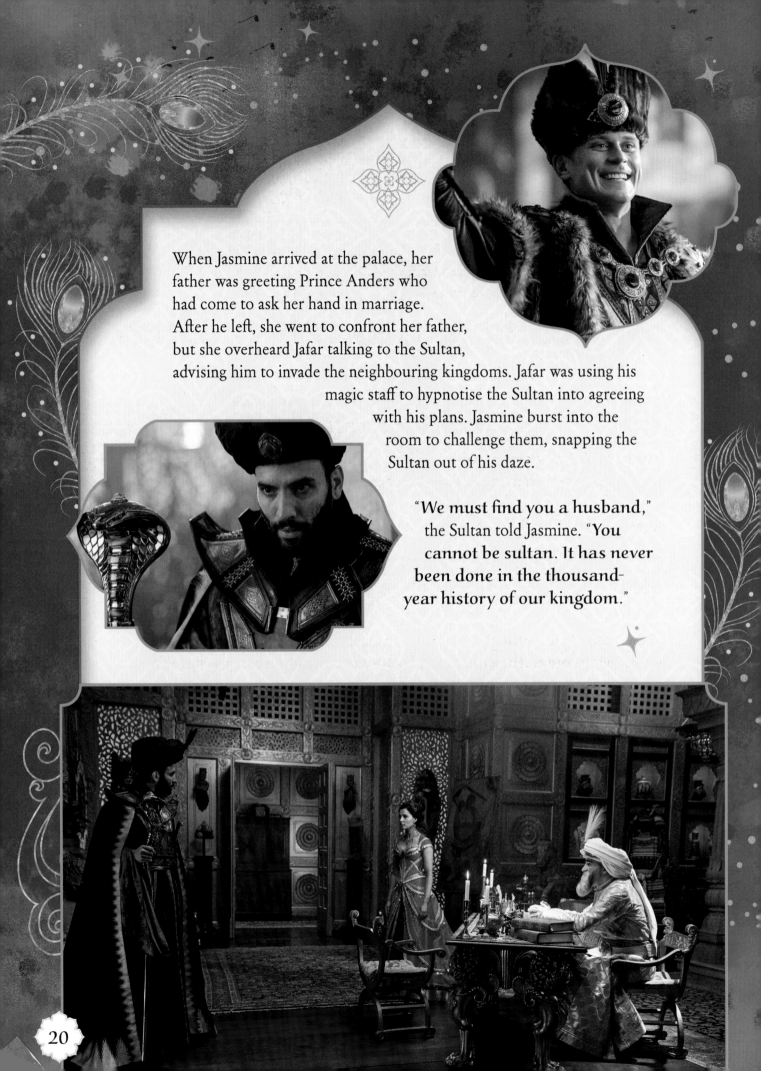

When Jasmine arrived at the palace, her father was greeting Prince Anders who had come to ask her hand in marriage. After he left, she went to confront her father, but she overheard Jafar talking to the Sultan, advising him to invade the neighbouring kingdoms. Jafar was using his magic staff to hypnotise the Sultan into agreeing with his plans. Jasmine burst into the room to challenge them, snapping the Sultan out of his daze.

"We must find you a husband," the Sultan told Jasmine. "You cannot be sultan. It has never been done in the thousand-year history of our kingdom."

Later that day, Jafar sat in his chambers with his pet parrot, Iago.

## "I need real power, I need the lamp" he raged.

The lamp had the power to take control of Agrabah for good, but he needed a thief to retrieve it from the Cave of Wonders for him.

Just then, Aladdin climbed over the palace walls. He quickly put on a servant's outfit and knocked on Jasmine's door.

"What are you doing here?" she asked.

"Returning your bracelet," Aladdin replied, clasping the bracelet to her wrist. "Meet me in the courtyard by the fountain tomorrow," he said, revealing the hairpin he had just taken from her hair.

Jasmine must get to the palace before Prince Anders arrives. Help her find the quickest path through the busy Agrabah streets.

# Don't Be Late

**START**

**FINISH**

Answer on page 69

# Creature Features

How well do you know Aladdin, Jasmine and Jafar's animal friends? Decide which facts are true and which are false.

1  Abu the monkey wears clothes.    True ☐  False ☐

2  Raja is a fearsome lion.    True ☐  False ☐

3  Abu is a skilled thief.    True ☐  False ☐

4  Iago is a brightly coloured canary.    True ☐  False ☐

5  Raja's fur is orange with black spots.    True ☐  False ☐

6  Abu is Aladdin's friend.    True ☐  False ☐

7  Raja is loyal to Jafar.    True ☐  False ☐

8  Iago is Dalia's best friend.    True ☐  False ☐

Answer on page 69

# Which Character are You?

**1 You would wish...**

A. to be somebody important ☐
B. to explore new worlds ☐
C. to be free ☐
D. to start a new life ☐

**2 Pick a sidekick!**

A. A monkey ☐
B. A tiger ☐
C. A magic carpet ☐
D. Your friends are all you need ☐

**3 People see you as...**

A. charismatic ☐
B. determined ☐
C. hilarious ☐
D. caring ☐

**4 At a party, you can be found...**

A. trying to impress the crowd ☐
B. searching for engaging conversations ☐
C. offering others advice ☐
D. hanging out with your best friend ☐

**5 You would like to live...**

A. somewhere with the one you love ☐
B. somewhere without high walls ☐
C. somewhere with lots of living space ☐
D. somewhere close to your family ☐

**6 Choose a signature colour.**

A. Purple ☐
B. Teal ☐
C. Blue ☐
D. Red ☐

**7 A good evening would include...**

A. taking a walk around town ☐
B. adventuring to new places ☐
C. doing your own thing ☐
D. grooming your cat ☐

## If you picked mostly As ... you're like *Aladdin!*

Like Aladdin, you wish others could see you for more than just what is on the surface. You might be a diamond in the rough, but your resilience, charm, and determination to help others make you a *trustworthy friend.*

## If you picked mostly Bs ... you're like *Jasmine!*

Like Jasmine, you want to *explore and learn* about the world beyond your home. You are a natural-born leader and won't let yourself be trapped by anyone's expectations.

## If you picked mostly Cs ...you're like *Genie!*

Like Genie, you are the person people go to for a *helping hand*. But while you are often the one getting your friends out of trouble, it would be nice to take some time for yourself. It's time to grant your own wishes!

## If you picked mostly Ds ... you're like *Dalia!*

Like Dalia, you will do anything for your friends. Sometimes you can get lost in the background, but your clever wit doesn't go unnoticed. You are *loyal to your friends*, and you aren't afraid to break a few rules to help the people closest to you.

# In the Shadows

Whose shadows are these? Draw lines to match them to the right characters below.

A

B

C

D

1

2

3

4

Answer on page 69

# Best Friends Forever

Jasmine and Dalia are almost like sisters! Take a close look at this picture for 30 seconds, then cover it and answer the questions below about the princess and her pal.

1. Is Dalia wearing her hair up or down?
2. What shape is the jewel in the centre of Jasmine's necklace?
3. What colour is the stripe on Dalia's veil?
4. How many rings is Jasmine wearing?
5. Are Dalia and Jasmine looking at each other?

# Part Two

Jafar had watched Aladdin and
Princess Jasmine's exchange and
seen Aladdin return the bracelet. He
thought that Aladdin must be the diamond in the rough who could get the
lamp. The guards arrested Aladdin and brought him to Jafar in the desert.

"I can make you rich," Jafar told Aladdin. "Rich enough
to impress a princess. One small favour is all I ask."

Aladdin hadn't realised Jasmine was a princess.
He really liked her, so he agreed to Jafar's plan.
All Aladdin had to do was enter the cave and
find the lamp.

Aladdin and Abu walked towards the cave.
As they got nearer, it transformed into into the mouth
of a lion which swept them into the heart of the cave.

The cave was full of more treasures
than Aladdin and Abu had ever seen.
Abu reached for a gem, but Aladdin
pulled him away and they fell backwards
onto a beautiful woven carpet.

Suddenly the carpet came alive, floating in the air.

"Abu, is this a magic carpet?" Aladdin
asked. The end of the carpet rose and
shook its tassels as if it was nodding.

Aladdin climbed deeper into the
cave, until he saw the glimmer of the
gold lamp. Just as he reached it, Abu
grabbed a jewel, unable to control his
greed. The cave walls split open pouring
red-hot lava everywhere. Luckily the magic
carpet was there to rescue them, and it flew
them both to the mouth of the cave.

Jafar was waiting for them there, but he refused
to help them until Aladdin threw him the
lamp. When Aladdin reached for Jafar's
hand, he stamped on it instead. Aladdin
and Abu fell back into the cave
as it began to collapse.

Aladdin sat up and looked around.
The hot lava had disappeared, melting
all the treasures on the way, but one
treasure remained – the lamp!

Aladdin held the lamp up,
wondering why Jafar
would want something so
worthless. He noticed
an engraving on the side and
rubbed at the dirt to read it better.
Suddenly, blue smoke burst from the lamp and
out came a huge blue genie!

Genie introduced himself to his new master, Aladdin.
He told Aladdin that all he had to do was rub the lamp and
he would grant him three wishes.

Aladdin didn't want to waste a wish on getting out of the
cave, so he slipped the lamp to Abu and said to Genie,

"I wish you to
get us out of
this cave."

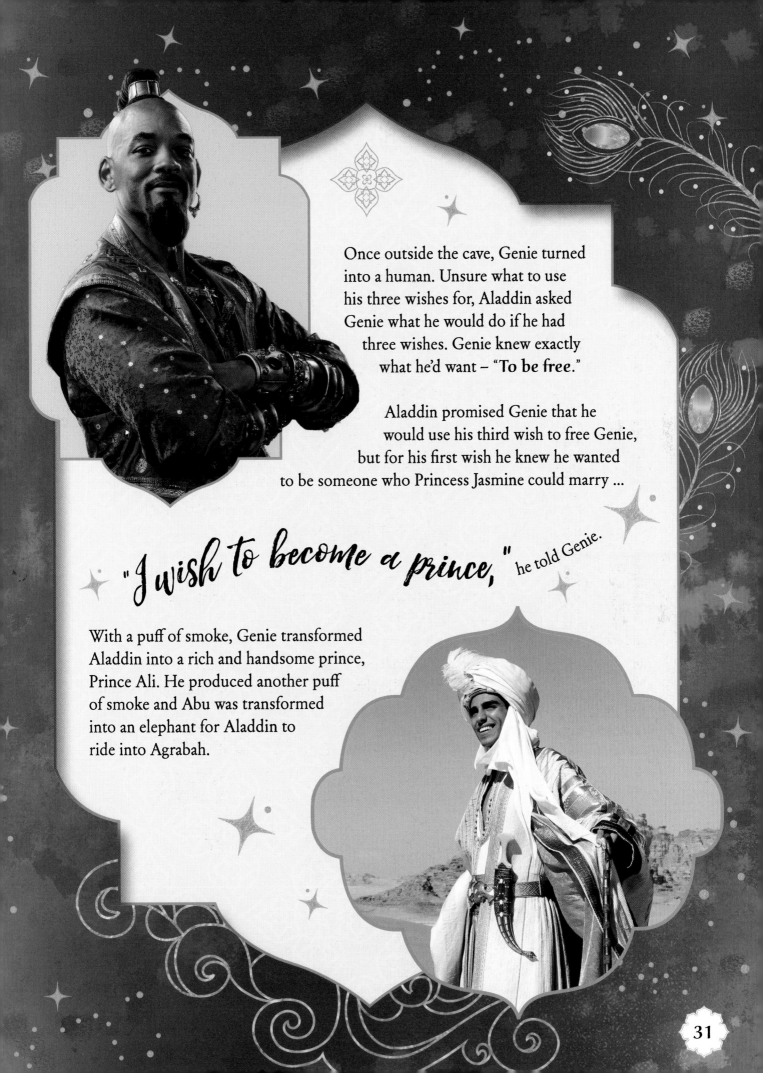

Once outside the cave, Genie turned into a human. Unsure what to use his three wishes for, Aladdin asked Genie what he would do if he had three wishes. Genie knew exactly what he'd want – **"To be free."**

Aladdin promised Genie that he would use his third wish to free Genie, but for his first wish he knew he wanted to be someone who Princess Jasmine could marry ...

*"I wish to become a prince,"* he told Genie.

With a puff of smoke, Genie transformed Aladdin into a rich and handsome prince, Prince Ali. He produced another puff of smoke and Abu was transformed into an elephant for Aladdin to ride into Agrabah.

31

# Finding Friends

Follow the tangled lines to find out what Aladdin, Genie and Jasmine are looking for. Write your answers below.

Aladdin is looking for ..................................................................

Genie is looking for ..................................................................

Jasmine is looking for ..................................................................

Answer on page 69

# In a Muddle

Can you unscramble the letters to reveal these characters' names? Write your answers in the boxes below.

D A L I N A D

**1** ☐☐☐☐☐☐☐☐

M E J A I N S

**2** ☐☐☐☐☐☐☐☐

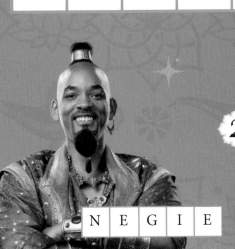

N E G I E

**3** ☐☐☐☐☐

A D I A L

**4** ☐☐☐☐☐☐

F A J R A

**5** ☐☐☐☐☐

Answer on page 69

# Design a Magic Carpet

The magic carpet is totally unique, but you can design your own one. Create a legendary carpet to fly away on.

DISNEY
Aladdin

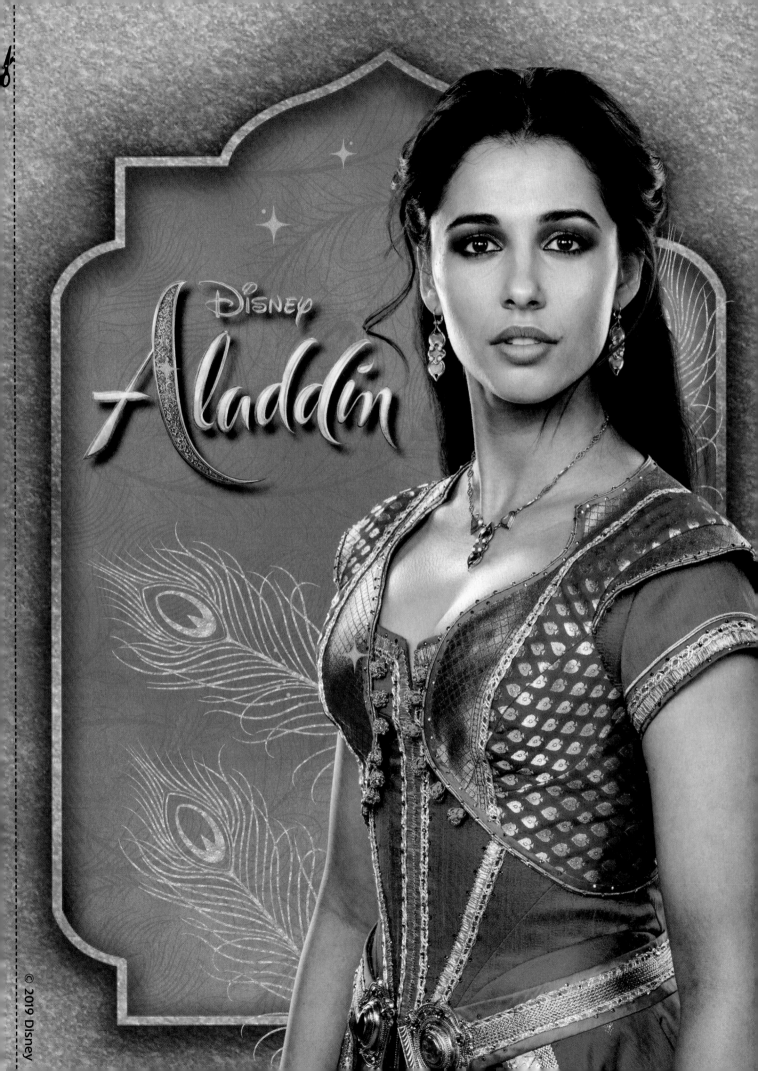

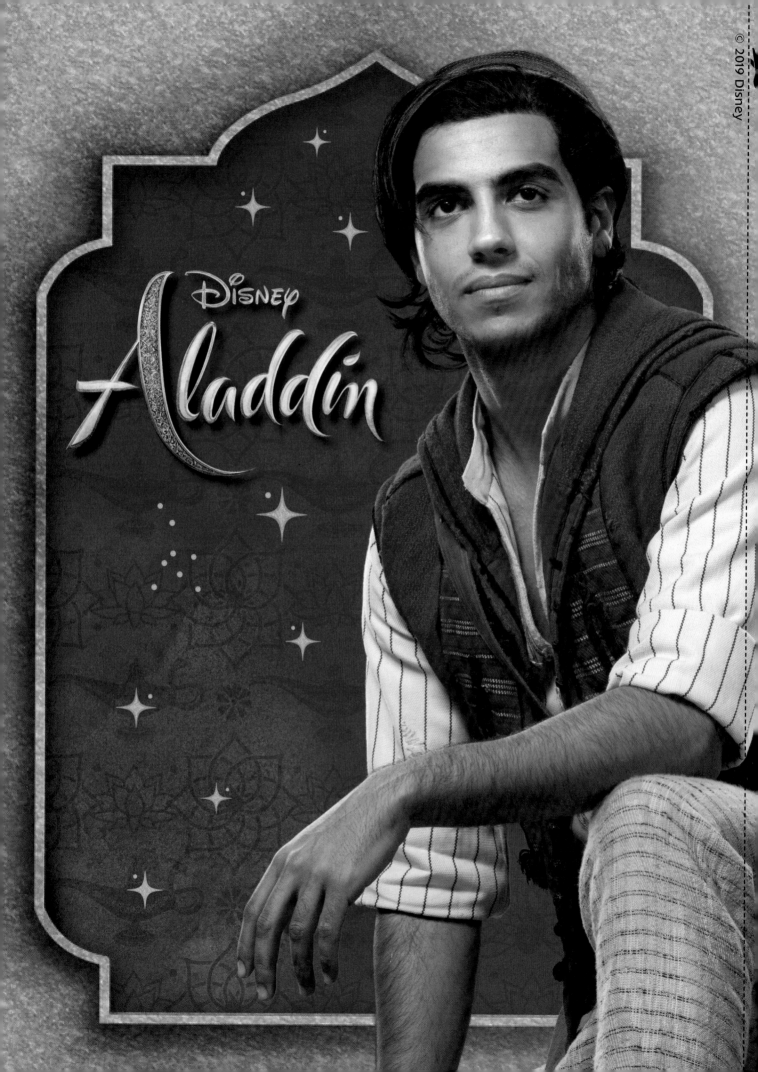

# Draw your Wishes

If you found a magic lamp with a genie inside, what would your three wishes be? Draw them below.

39

# Part Three

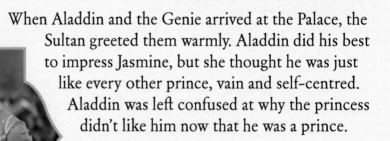

Genie led Aladdin into the city with a parade of dancers, musicians and soldiers conjured up by his magic.

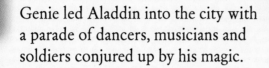

When Aladdin and the Genie arrived at the Palace, the Sultan greeted them warmly. Aladdin did his best to impress Jasmine, but she thought he was just like every other prince, vain and self-centred. Aladdin was left confused at why the princess didn't like him now that he was a prince.

Later that night, he tried to impress her at the Harvest Festival, but as soon as he started showing off, Jasmine was disappointed. He was just another arrogant prince after all.

After the festival, Aladdin sat in his guest chambers staring out of the window at Jasmine's room.

"You have to get me over there." He told Genie.

"Is that an official wish?" Genie asked.

"No," said Aladdin. "It's a favour. For a friend."

Genie had never had a friend before, and Aladdin had been kind to him. He decided to help him, and so he distracted Dalia so that Aladdin could sneak onto Jasmine's balcony.

Aladdin apologised to the princess for his behaviour. Seeing he was truly sorry, Jasmine forgave him and confessed that she was jealous of a prince like him, getting to travel the world and meet new people.

"I'd think a princess could go everywhere," Aladdin told her.

"Not this Princess," she replied.

Aladdin had an idea. He leapt off the balcony onto the magic carpet and floated back up to Jasmine who stood there in shock.

"Do you trust me?" he asked her.

Jasmine had been asked that before by the boy in the market. Could Prince Ali have been that boy? She stepped onto the carpet and they flew away on an adventure all over Agrabah and beyond...

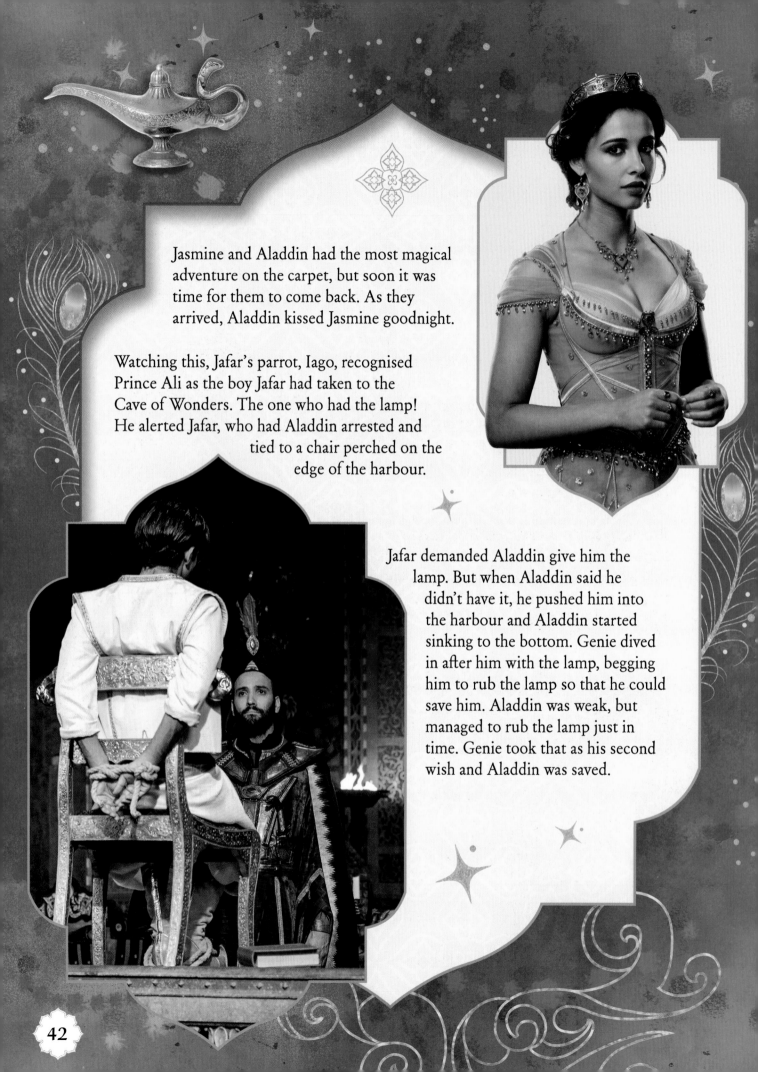

Jasmine and Aladdin had the most magical adventure on the carpet, but soon it was time for them to come back. As they arrived, Aladdin kissed Jasmine goodnight.

Watching this, Jafar's parrot, Iago, recognised Prince Ali as the boy Jafar had taken to the Cave of Wonders. The one who had the lamp! He alerted Jafar, who had Aladdin arrested and tied to a chair perched on the edge of the harbour.

Jafar demanded Aladdin give him the lamp. But when Aladdin said he didn't have it, he pushed him into the harbour and Aladdin started sinking to the bottom. Genie dived in after him with the lamp, begging him to rub the lamp so that he could save him. Aladdin was weak, but managed to rub the lamp just in time. Genie took that as his second wish and Aladdin was saved.

After the incident, Aladdin wanted to tell the Sultan about Jafar's treachery, but when he arrived, he found the Sultan in a daze. Genie realised that Jafar was hypnotising him and Aladdin grabbed Jafar's staff, smashing it on the floor. The Sultan was free from the spell and ordered his guards to lock Jafar in the dungeon.

Back in the guest chambers, Genie asked Aladdin why he didn't tell Jasmine the truth.

"People like me don't get anything except by pretending," Aladdin replied.

Unsure what to do, Aladdin went to the secret tower. But he bumped into a beggar on the way, who stole the lamp from his pocket without him realising. The beggar wasn't just anyone, it was Jafar in disguise!

Jafar rubbed the lamp and said,

*"I wish to be Sultan of Agrabah!"*

# Design a Map

Jasmine loves to read and study maps, but couldn't find Prince Ali's kingdom of Ababwa. Does it exist? Draw what you imagine Ababwa would look like on a map.

# Lots of Lamps

The Genie lives inside the magic lamp, but which one is it? Draw lines to connect the pairs of lamps. The one that isn't part of a pair is the Genie's lamp.

A

B

C

D

E

F

G

H

I

Answer on page 69

# A Surprise Visit

Aladdin needs to return Jasmine's bracelet. Help him follow the path and sneak past the palace guards so he can prove he is not a thief.

**Start**

**2**

**3**
Stop to listen at the palace door. Miss a turn.

**4**

**18**

**19**

**20**

**21**
Wait until Jafar has gone. Miss a turn.

**17**

**16**
A guard is coming! Go back 2 spaces.

**15**

**14**

# How to play:
## You will need counters/coins and a dice

With a friend, choose which colour counter you'd like to play with.
Then take turns rolling the die and moving around the board the same
number of spaces as the number thrown. If you land on an instruction space,
do what it says. The first player to reach the finish is the winner!

**5**

**6**

**7**
Creep along
the corridor.
Move forward
2 spaces.

**8**

**22**

**23**

**24**
Finish

**9**

**13**

**12**

**11**

**10**
Find a magic carpet.
Take another turn.

# Who Said What?

There are many memorable lines spoken in the film, but can you remember who said what?

**Aladdin**

**Jasmine**

**Dalia**

**Genie**

**Jafar**

**1** Why would we invade my mother's kingdom?

**2** Is that an official wish?

**3** I think this one's different.

**4** I wish to be the sultan of Agrabah!

**5** You're only in trouble if you get caught!

Answer on page 69

# In the Clouds

Aladdin and Jasmine have spotted some familiar shapes in the clouds.

**What can you see in the sky?**
**Write down the shapes on the lines below.**

..........................................................................
..........................................................................
..........................................................................
..........................................................................
..........................................................................
..........................................................................
..........................................................................

# Part Four

Jafar's first order as Sultan was to invade the neighbouring kingdom of Shirabad, starting a war. But Princess Jasmine convinced the palace guards not to allow his commands. With them no longer on his side, Jafar made his second wish.

## "I wish to become the most powerful sorcerer there is!"

In his tower hideaway, Aladdin realised he didn't have the lamp anymore. He rushed to the palace, and when he arrived, Jafar used his new powers to reveal Aladdin as a street rat. Jasmine was in shock. He had lied about who he really was.

Before Aladdin could stop him, Jafar used his magic to send Aladdin and Abu to an icy tundra miles away from Agrabah. Without their help, Jasmine was forced to agree to marry Jafar. But just as the wedding began, Aladdin arrived on the magic carpet and rescued Jasmine and the lamp.

Not wanting to let Aladdin get away, Jafar summoned a vicious storm. Lightning hit the magic carpet and the trio were pulled back to Agrabah and into Jafar's clutches.

Aladdin and Jasmine approached Jafar. They were no longer afraid of him. "You can't find what you're looking for in that lamp. I tried and failed, and so will you!" shouted Aladdin.

"You think so?" laughed Jafar, "I am the greatest sorcerer the world has ever seen!"

Aladdin shook his head. "You'll never have more power than the Genie," he told Jafar.

Jafar rubbed the lamp and wished to be the most powerful person in the world - to be a genie.

Genie grinned, realising that Jafar had been set up. He turned him into a powerful genie, but Jafar couldn't use his magic.

"A genie without a master goes in the lamp," Aladdin told Jafar, as he was sucked into the lamp. Jafar was defeated.

The Sultan was finally free of Jafar and he had realised that his daughter was much stronger than he had thought. "You will be our next sultan and rule over Agrabah," he told her.

Seeing the Sultan and Jasmine reunited, Aladdin turned to Genie to make his final wish.

*"I wish to set you free, Genie"* he said.

Genie was overwhelmed by Aladdin's wish. He was finally free. He turned back into a man and thanked Aladdin with a hug. They both knew that they were true friends.

As Aladdin turned to leave, Jasmine called "Stop, thief!"

Aladdin turned to see her holding up her half of the hairpin that he had taken earlier. He smiled as he presented her with the other half. Jasmine told him that as the future sultan she had decided that she would marry whoever she wanted ... even a thief.

# Questions About the Story

How well do you remember the story?
Tick the correct answers to these questions about it.

**1. Who saves Princess Jasmine from the angry stallholder in the marketplace?**

A Aladdin ☐     B Jafar ☐

**2. Who is the prince who comes to marry Princess Jasmine?**

A Prince Charming ☐     B Prince Anders ☐

**3. What two items do Aladdin and Abu steal from Princess Jasmine?**

A A bracelet and half a hairpin ☐     B A necklace and a hairband ☐

**4. How does Aladdin convince Genie to get them out of the Cave of Wonders?**

A He tricks him into thinking it's one of his wishes ☐     B He digs a hole with Abu ☐

**5. At what party do Aladdin and Jasmine dance together?**

A The Sultan's birthday party ☐     B The Harvest Festival ☐

**6. How does Jafar hypnotise the Sultan?**

A With his snake staff ☐     B With a spinning clock ☐

**7. What is Jafar's second wish?**

A To be the Sultan of Agrabah ☐     B To be the most powerful sorcerer in the land ☐

**8. Whose wish to be free is granted?**

A Princess Jasmine ☐     B Genie ☐

# Serpent's Puzzle

sssssssssssgsssssssss

Jafar's symbol is the snake. Follow the snake, crossing off every 'S' and copying the remaining letters into the boxes to reveal what he wants most.

What Jafar wants most is:

☐☐☐☐☐ ☐☐☐☐☐

Answer on page 69

54

# Make your own Cobra Staff

You will need:
Coloured pens
A jewel sticker (optional)
Thick paper
Tape
Scissors
A pencil

**1**

Draw the shape of your cobra staff. It should be 1.5 times the length of your pencil, and 3 times the width of your pencil.

**2**

Decorate both sides of your cobra staff. The outside should have the cobra's face and a circle for your jewel.

**3**

Place your pencil onto the inside of the paper, and carefully roll the sides around the pencil. Then use tape to hold it in place.

**4**

Carefully create a hook shape by bending the paper over so that your snake is facing forward.

**5**

Using the tape, apply your jewel into the circle on the top of your staff. Your cobra staff is now ready!

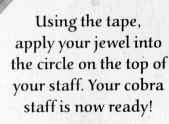

# Royal Rooms

Inside the Palace, the rooms are filled with objects. Take a look around and see if you can spot the precious items in the scene.

Two ornate chairs     Some candlesticks     Two helmets

A red book     A large white feather     A painting

Answer on page 69

# Sparkling Sums

The Sultan is counting up his jewels. Complete the sums to see how many jewels of each colour he has.

$$3 + 5 + 1 = \boxed{\phantom{00}}$$

$$6 + 4 + 2 = \boxed{\phantom{00}}$$

$$4 + 6 + 1 = \boxed{\phantom{00}}$$

$$4 + 5 + 3 = \boxed{\phantom{00}}$$

$$2 + 6 + 4 = \boxed{\phantom{00}}$$

Answer on page 69

# Colourful Princess

Jasmine has a colourful personality and she wears colourful clothes to match! Link the colours to wherever they appear in her dresses.

Orange ◆ Purple ◆ Green ◆ Pink ◆ Red ◆ Yellow ◆ Blue ◆ Teal ◆ Gold

# Wonderful Wordsearch

Can you find all of these words in the puzzle below?

| | | | |
|---|---|---|---|
| ABU | DALIA | JASMINE | QUEEN |
| ALADDIN | IAGO | PRINCE | RAJA |
| CARPET | JAFAR | LAMP | SULTAN |

|   |   |   |   |   |   |   |   |   |   |   |   |
|---|---|---|---|---|---|---|---|---|---|---|---|
|   |   |   |   | U | D | H | R | A | J | A | L | Q |
| P | A | B |   |   | T | C | A | N | A | H | K | U |
| O | I | M | Q | T |   | M | P | T | F | C | S | E |
| C | A | N | L | A | M | P |   | H | A | L | V | E |
| O | L | O | E | R | Z | E |   | S | R | F | S | N |
| C | A | R | P | E | T | E | S | T | F | K | M | D |
| u | D | O | R | R | E | J | A | L | I | A | B | S |
| M | D | I | L | R | D | A | L | A | A | C | u |   |
| N | I | u | M | I | D | S | L | G | O | D | L |   |
| S | N | X | T | T | L | M | A | E | O | B | F | T |
| S | P | L | M | A | A | I | N | T | B | E | T | A |
| N | A | L | P | A | L | N | E | E | R | T | M | N |
| I | P | R | I | N | C | E | R |   |   |   |   |   |

Answer on page 69

# Crack the Code

Genie has written a secret message to Dalia. What does it say? Use the key to reveal the answer.

— — — — — —          — — — — —

— — — — — — — — —

**Key:**

| A | D | E | G | H | I | M | N | R | T |
|---|---|---|---|---|---|---|---|---|---|

Answer on page 69

# Secret Identities

In Agrabah, nothing is as it seems. Can you unscramble this movie trivia?

1. Jasmine tells Aladdin her name is . . . LIAAD

2. Before setting foot in Agrabah,
Genie transforms into a . . . MUAHN

3. Dalia helps Jasmine escape from the . . . ACPEAL

4. The palace guards think Aladdin is
nothing but a . . . ETTRES TAR

5. The lamp is found in the Cave of . . . RONDEWS

6. Aladdin takes on an alter ego as . . . RNCEPI LAI

Answer on page 69

61

# Who Wore What?

See if you can match the characters to the right clothing items.

**A**

**B**

**C**

**D**

**E**

**F**

**G**

**1**

**2**

**3**

**4**

**5**

**6**

**7**

Answer on page 69

# Genie's Got Moves

A  B  C

Can you work out which move Genie will do next? Write the letters in the boxes to complete the pattern in each row.

1

2

3

4

# Quiz Time!

How well do you know Aladdin and Jasmine? Tick the correct picture to answer each question.

**1** Who is being pressured to get married?

**2** Whose sidekick is Abu?

**3** Who finds the magic lamp?

**4** Whose father is the Sultan of Agrabah?

**5** Who has a pet tiger called Raja?

**6** Who wishes for the Genie to be set free?

Answer on page 69

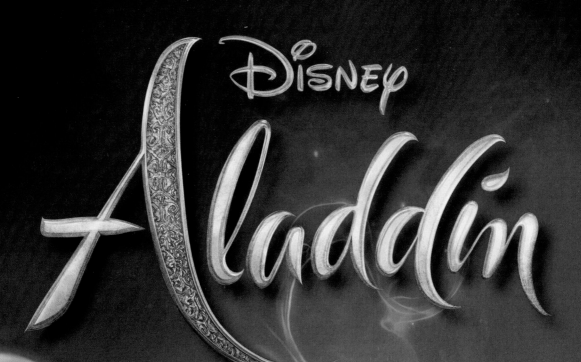

# Twisted Sorcery

If the Sultan had seen Jafar's lair, he may have known Jafar was up to no good. What would others find in your secret lair? Draw it below.

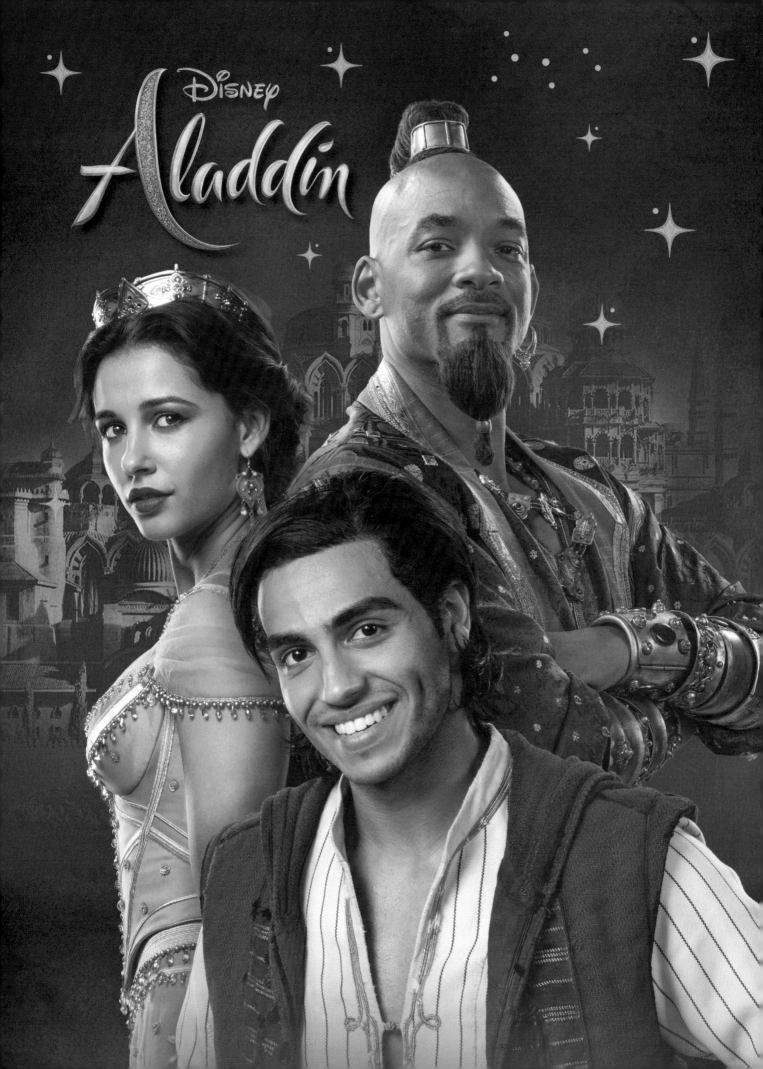

# Answers

**Page 9 Magic Carpet Ride**
2

**Page 13 Mystical Shadows**
Shadow E

**Page 15 Sorcerer's Sudoku**

1
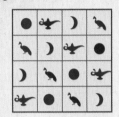

2

3
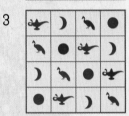

**Page 22 Don't be late**

**Page 23 Creature Features**
1. True; 2. False; 3. True;
4. False; 5. False; 6. True;
7. False; 8. False

**Page 26 In the Shadows**
A–3, B–4, C–2, D–1

**Page 27 Best Friends Forever**
1–Down
2–Heart-shaped
3–Red
4–Two
5–No

**Page 33 In a Muddle**
1. Aladdin; 2. Jasmine;
3. Genie; 4. Dalia; 5. Jafar

**Page 44 Finding Friends**
Aladdin is looking for Abu.
Jasmine is looking for Raja.
Genie is looking for the magic lamp

**Page 45 Lots of Lamps**
A–H, B–G, D–F, E–I, C is the Genie's lamp.

**Page 48 Who Said What?**
1. Jasmine; 2. Genie; 3. Dalia;
4. Jafar; 5. Aladdin

**Page 49 In the Clouds**
A teapot, the magic lamp, an apple,
a necklace, a palm tree, a vase, a camel

**Page 53 Questions About the Story**
1–A, 2–B, 3–A, 4–A, 5–B, 6–A, 7–B, 8–B.

**Page 54 Serpent's Puzzle**
GREAT POWER

**Page 56 Royal Rooms**

**Page 57 Sparkling Sums**
Red–9; Blue–13; Yellow–11;
Green–15; Purple–12

**Page 58 Colourful Princess**
A–Teal, Purple, Yellow, Gold
B–Teal, Gold
C–Teal, Pink, Gold, Green
D–Orange, Yellow, Green

**Page 59 Wonderful Wordsearch**

| P | A | B | U | D | H | R | A | J | A | L | Q |
|---|---|---|---|---|---|---|---|---|---|---|---|
| O | I | M | Q | T | C | A | N | A | H | K | U |
| C | A | N | L | A | M | P | T | F | C | S | E |
| O | L | O | E | R | Z | E | H | A | L | V | E |
| C | A | R | P | E | T | E | S | R | F | S | N |
| U | D | O | R | R | E | J | T | F | K | M | D |
| M | D | I | L | R | D | A | L | I | A | B | S |
| N | I | U | M | I | D | S | L | A | A | C | U |
| S | N | X | T | T | L | M | A | G | O | D | L |
| S | P | L | M | A | A | I | E | O | B | F | T |
| N | A | L | P | A | L | N | T | B | E | T | A |
| I | P | R | I | N | C | E | E | R | T | M | N |

**Page 60 Crack the Code**
MEET ME IN THE GARDEN

**Page 61 Secret Identities**
1. Dalia; 2. Human; 3. Palace; 4. Street Rat;
5. Wonders; 6. Prince Ali

**Page 62 Who Wore What?**
A–3, B–7, C–4, D–6, E–5, F–2, G–1

**Page 63 Genie's Got Moves**
1–B; 2–C; 3–C; 4–B

**Page 64 Quiz Time!**
1. Jasmine; 2. Aladdin; 3. Aladdin;
4. Jasmine; 5. Jasmine; 6. Aladdin